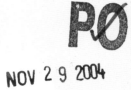

James Edgar
and
Jean Jessop Hervey
Point Loma Branch Library

California
on my mind

" *Everything worth photographing is in California.* "

Edward Weston
from *Picturing California:*
A Century of Photographic Genius

James Edgar
and
Jean Jessop Hervey

FALCON™

Ocotillo and brittlebush add splashes of color to Anza-Borrego Desert State Park, California's largest state park JAMES RANDKLEV

" I have found that in the summer I am intensely aware of every facet of the desert. The white light of noon saturates each stone and leaf so they are drained of color and seem almost transparent. The silence makes itself heard as a sort of subliminal humming from deep within the rocks and hills. I amuse myself by imagining that what I hear is the fabric of the universe making the tiny molecular adjustments that knit the whole shebang together. "

Harry Daniel
Chairman, Anza-Borrego Desert
Natural History Association, July 1982
from *Anza-Borrego Desert State Park*

Black-tailed jackrabbit JEFF FOOTT

3

A rock pinnacle and its image in Minaret Lake high in the Ansel Adams Wilderness of the Sierra Nevada   LONDIE PADELSKY

Nevada Falls roars down the striated shoulder of Liberty Cap in Yosemite National Park   LONDIE PADELSKY

An early spring sunset highlights the rocks at Point Pinos on the Monterey Peninsula   JEFF GNASS

“Where the far edge of California gives way to the ocean, landscape shifts to seascape . . . a confrontation of the two great worlds supported by our planet. Beaches fringe a restless surf; headlands thrust obstinately into churning swells; and islets persist in spite of the sea's aggression. These are outposts of California, stubborn and steadfast. ”

Elna S. Bakker
An Island Called California

A lined shore crab hiding in a tidepool crevice   JEFF FOOTT

A cypress's twisting branches rise above the Cypress Grove Trail at Point Lobos State Reserve TERRY DONNELLY

Moss-covered stones slow the path of a waterfall on the Cataract Trail in Marin County   MICHAEL EVAN SEWELL

Cala lilies follow a rivulet down to Abalone Cove in Garrapata State Park   LARRY ULRICH

The incredible geology of Devils Postpile National Monument: the hexagonal columns of rock fractured off a cooling flow of basaltic lava then were toppled by a large glacier   CHRISTOPHER TALBOT FRANK

"California remains a stirring reality, even if its ecology struggles to keep up with the mythology. It is still wild in many places; its beauty is robust, not yet tamed by being photographed."

David Thomson
Driving in a Back Projection

The South and Middle forks of the Smith River meet on a cool morning in Six Rivers National Forest LARRY ULRICH

Fall in the Sierra Nevada brings out a fiery range of color in the aspens on Grant Lake   CHRISTOPHER TALBOT FRANK

A western tanager brightens the greens of a mountain forest   DONALD M. JONES

Winter ferns and thimbleberry brush against the feet of giants along the Generals Highway in Sequoia National Park LARRY ULRICH

Skiers carving graceful turns above the sapphire surface of Lake Tahoe, the continent's third deepest lake, at Homewood Ski Area   FRANK S. BALTHIS

> *Every winter the High Sierra and the middle forest region get snow in glorious abundance, and even the foot-hills are at times whitened. Then all the range looks like a vast beveled wall of purest marble.*

John Muir
The Mountains of California

Over the edge: snowboarder at Donner Summit LARRY PROSOR

Cross-country skiers revel in fresh snow among the lodgepole pines at Mount Pinos, Los Padres National Forest JAMES RANDKLEV

The open slopes of Squaw Valley entice alpine skiers from all over the world   FRANK S. BALTHIS

Sledding up a storm in the Sierra Nevada   LARRY PROSOR

A century plant stands before the centuries-old bell tower of Mission San Diego de Alcala LARRY ULRICH

A Carmel sunrise highlights the church front in the cool courtyard of Mission San Carlos Borromeo del Rio Carmelo   LARRY ULRICH

The handcrafted brick archway and gate leading to the
Mission San Juan Capistrano bell wall   TERRY DONNELLY

*“ Missions, my lord, missions—that
is what this country needs. ”*

Father Junípero Serra, ca. 1780

Light and shadow on the Humboldt coast: a swirling sunset reflects on calm Trinidad Bay at Tepona Point Beach   JEFF GNASS

A hang glider taking off from the headland at
Torrey Pines State Reserve   CHUCK PLACE

At Trinidad Bay, California poppies vie with the Memorial Lighthouse for the eye's attention LARRY ULRICH

Los Angeles's library tower and Bonaventure Hotel glow above an entrance to downtown's 110 Freeway KATHLEEN NORRIS COOK

Rodeo Drive in Beverly Hills: the famous shopping grounds of the wealthy   KERRICK JAMES

Crossing in style: Rodeo Drive   KERRICK JAMES

❝ In all the world, there neither was nor would there ever be another place like this City of the Angels. Here the American people were erupting, like lava from a volcano. . . .❞

Carey McWilliams
Southern California Country

A Hollywood mural of the stars gathered to watch us   KERRICK JAMES

The Duke's star graces Hollywood's Walk of Fame
PAULA BORCHARDT

Perhaps the most famous southern California landmark
KERRICK JAMES

The recently restored 1901 Angel's Flight funicular railway carries passengers one steep block, from Grand Central Market to the downtown skyscrapers, for a mere twenty-five cents PAULA BORCHARDT

A new generation makes friends with Disneyland's best-known resident JAMES KURT GARDNER

Queen Mary at dusk: the retired Cunard ocean liner regally lit at Long Beach Harbor   JEFF GNASS

Setting sail for the pleasures of childhood at San Diego's Sea World
DENNIS SHIRTCLIFF/FREEZE FRAME WEST

The oak-studded hillsides of Malibu host a huge gathering of lupines each summer   JAMES RANDKLEV

66 The whole valley floor, and the foothills too, would be carpeted with lupins and poppies. Once a woman told me that colored flowers would seem more bright if you added a few white flowers to give the colors definition. Every petal of blue lupin is edged with white, so that a field of lupins is more blue than you can imagine. And mixed with these were splashes of California poppies. These too are of a burning color—not orange, not gold, but if pure gold were liquid and could raise a cream, that golden cream might be like the color of the poppies. 99

John Steinbeck
East of Eden

Radiant flowers at Temblor Range dazzle two young flower-gatherers
LONDIE PADELSKY

A carpet of California poppies, cream cups, and goldfields rolled out before a stand of valley oak at Diablo Range in Fresno County LARRY ULRICH

Mount Whitney's 14,495-foot summit, the highest point in the Lower 48, resembles an alien landscape   LARRY CARVER

> **❝** *This is the true Mount Whitney. . . . It stands, not like white Shasta, in a grandeur of solitude, but about it gather companies of crag and spire, piercing the blue or wrapped in monkish raiment of snowstorm and mist. . . . Silence reigns on these icy heights, save when the scream of Sierra eagle or loud crescendo of avalanche interrupts the frozen stillness, or when in symphonic fullness a storm rolls through vacant canyons. . . .* **❞**

Clarence King
Mount Whitney

A wary coyote in Death Valley LONDIE PADELSKY

The world's oldest living trees grow atop the White Mountains in the Ancient Bristlecone Pine Forest DENNIS FLAHERTY

"Death Valley, from ten thousand feet on a warm September afternoon, elongates flat and arid, stained with thin patches of vegetation, bound by mountains, smudged with cloud shadows that mottle it like Carrara marble. . . . Green would seem out of place here. Green symbolizes flickering leaves, gentle sounds, quiet dusks. But this rocky landscape is silent, immutable, changing not in the span of our eyesight. . . ."

Ann Haymond Zwinger
The Mysterious Lands

A boulder seems to rest in its mysterious tracks at Death Valley's Racetrack Playa STEVE MOHLENKAMP

Raven tracks head toward the Last Chance Mountains in Death Valley National Park's Eureka Sand Dunes JACK DYKINGA

> *Half a dozen little mountain brooks flow into Mono Lake, but not a stream of any kind flows out of it. It neither rises nor falls, apparently, and what it does with its surplus water is a dark and bloody mystery.*

Mark Twain
Roughing It

Great egret at Los Banos National Wildlife Refuge MIKE A. ANICH

The surface of Mono Lake reflects sunset clouds and strange formations of tufa (porous limestone)   CHRISTOPHER TALBOT FRANK

Morning sun highlights the desert flora against a purple sky at Southwest Palm Grove in Anza-Borrego Desert State Park   JEFF GNASS

A desert tortoise rests at the entrance to its burrow in
Joshua Tree National Park   JEFF FOOTT

The Providence Mountains strike a pose behind a blooming yucca in the Mojave National Preserve LARRY ULRICH

Desert bighorn sheep TOM AND PAT LEESON

Lone Pine Peak, at 12,944 feet, stands majestically above the Sierra Nevada ERIC WUNROW

66 *Every rock seems to glow with life.*
Some lean back in majestic repose;
others, absolutely sheer, or nearly so,
for thousands of feet, advance their
brows in thoughtful attitudes beyond
their companions, giving welcome to
storms and calms alike, seemingly
conscious yet heedless of everything
going on about them . . . their feet set
in pine-groves and gay emerald
meadows, their brows in the sky;
bathed in light, bathed in floods of
singing water. . . . 99

John Muir
The Mountains of California

Glacier-polished spires of ancient granite at Castle Crags State Park
MICHAEL EVAN SEWELL

Water rushing out of Thousand Islands Lake in front of Banner Peak, Ansel Adams Wilderness   LARRY ULRICH

A majestic tule elk bull, a species unique to California, tests the wind   GARY R. ZAHM

❝ *As our population grows, we feel the need to be in wilderness.*
The quality of our experiences in the canyons draws us back to
renew our spirits . . . now excitement and challenge, now gentle
solitude, a moment's exchange with a deer or a heron or a flicker
or an otter. ❞

Stan Padilla
The American River

High in the Cascade Range, the McCloud River flows past delicate bouquets of Indian rhubarb
in a California Nature Conservancy Preserve LARRY ULRICH

Mist-shrouded redwoods towering above a ground cover of Douglas' iris and ferns in Redwood National Park CHUCK PLACE

When a tree takes a notion to grow in California nothing in heaven or on earth will stop it. **"**

Lilian Leland
Travelling Alone,
A Woman's Journey Round the World

A bobcat resting in a meadow MIKE ANICH

Giant sequoias are found in scattered groves on western slopes of the Sierra Nevada, especially in Sequoia National Park   STEVE MOHLENKAMP

With a base circumference of 108 feet, the General Grant sequoia in Kings Canyon National Park is the second largest tree in the world ERIC WUNROW

A backpacker and his dog hoping for a bite at Lundy Lake Canyon in the Inyo National Forest, Sierra Nevada   LONDIE PADELSKY

❝ As we are becoming more hemmed in by our highly technological society, these moments in wilderness reconnect us to the beauty and the complexity of our natural world. We can take a moment to breathe freely, to think and dream, and to be grateful for the beauty all around us . . . ❞

Stan Padilla
The American River

Mountain bikers enjoy the final moments of another perfect California day   LARRY PROSOR

Paddling the reeds: a grand day on Sierra Lake, west of Highway 395 in Mono County   LONDIE PADELSKY

The sheer wall of Half Dome, the tallest and most recognizable of Yosemite's monoliths, basks in a sunset glow LARRY ULRICH

&6 *Go where you may within the bounds of California, mountains are ever in sight, charming and glorifying every landscape.* **99**

John Muir
The Mountains of California

A bungee-jumper takes off at Squaw Valley LARRY PROSOR

Hanging on with bare fingers, a climber is doused by Upper Yosemite Falls in its 2,430-foot plunge to the floor of Yosemite Valley
GALEN ROWELL/MOUNTAIN LIGHT PHOTOGRAPHY

Spectacular cliffs and sunsets first drew artists to the Laguna Beach coastline in the 1890s.
Today festivals and galleries prosper year-round amid the palm trees   FRANK S. BALTHIS

> *"... this strip of coast, this tiny region, seems to be looking westward across the Pacific, waiting for the future that one can somehow sense, and feel, and see."*
>
> Carey McWilliams
> *Southern California Country*

Surf and sand inspire creativity at Big Sur MARK GIBSON

A surfer kicks out, enjoying a very California form of recreation   ROB GILLEY

> *It is the beach that fuses all the images together, of an easy way of life, a freedom to do—what? To be a beach bum out in California: off-road bike, surf board, gliding on the palisades, water-skiing in the bay. Blond hair, tan skin, strong white teeth, and big, metallic music throbbing across the sand.* **"**

Richard Reinhardt
California From the Air

Catching up on the news at Red's in San Francisco   LARRY PROSOR

Shooting the tube, the ultimate wave riding maneuver   ROB GILLEY

California girls and beach scenes like this make you feel like you've stepped into a Beach Boys song   ROB GILLEY

Labor Day crowds converge on Huntington Beach   ROB GILLEY

Now an official Olympic sport, beach volleyball has long been a crowd-pleaser   ROB GILLEY

Running along the shore at sunset: hard, happy work   LARRY PROSOR

Weight training at Venice Beach: for most, a spectator sport   MARK E. GIBSON

A newly discovered species, this giant purple jellyfish was photographed off the shore of San Diego BOB CRANSTON

Shrimp and a moray eel, Coronado Island RANDY MORSE/TOM STACK & ASSOCIATES

A starfish and a garibaldi search for food in a kelp forest at Point Loma BOB CRANSTON

The kelp exhibit tank at La Jolla's Stephen Birch Aquarium works its aquatic magic on a group of schoolchildren   STEPHEN SIMPSON

A hermit crab perches on a tidepool rock in Monterey Bay
JEFF FOOTT

A bat star clings to a patch of sea lettuce
in a Monterey Bay tidepool JEFF FOOTT

The surf-swept arc of Pismo Beach draws clam lovers from near and far; most of the clam beds are protected in a preserve FRANK S. BALTHIS

A vineyard in the Valley of the Moon, Sonoma County, offers roses and wine to the romantic visitor FRANK S. BALTHIS

A young vineyard worker adding his pickings to the trough FRANK S. BALTHIS

Gleaming casks: golden oak enhances the wine in the cellars of Sebastiani Vineyards ED COOPER

Cabernet Sauvignon wine grapes ED COOPER

California Chardonnay wine grapes ED COOPER

The Santa Lucia Mountains provide a gentle backdrop for this budding lettuce crop near San Luis Obispo LONDIE PADELSKY

They drove through Tehachapi in the morning glow, and the sun came up behind them, and then—suddenly they saw the great valley below them. . . . The vineyards, the orchards, the great flat valley, green and beautiful, the trees set in rows, and the farm houses. . . .

Pa sighed, 'I never knowed there was anything like her.' The peach trees and the walnut groves, and the dark green patches of oranges. And red roofs among the trees, and barns—rich barns. . . .

Ruthie and Winfield scrambled down from the car, and they stood, silent and awestruck, embarassed before the great valley. The distance was thinned with haze, and the land grew softer and softer in the distance. A windmill flashed in the sun, and its turning blades were like a little heliograph, far away. Ruthie and Winfield looked at it, and Ruthie whispered, 'It's California.'

John Steinbeck
The Grapes of Wrath

A young picker with the fruits of her labor in a San Luis Obispo strawberry field   LONDIE PADELSKY

Sorting cattle at Miller and Wood Ranch near Crowley Lake   LONDIE PADELSKY

> 66 *I didn't choose ranching. I was born to it.*
> *A person almost has to be, because ranching*
> *isn't a job. It's a way of life. . . . A person really*
> *has to love what he is doing to live with that*
> *commitment, and I do. . . . How many people*
> *on Wall Street have the view from their offices*
> *that ranchers have from theirs?* 99

Mark J. Lacey, Lacey & Son Cattle Ranches
from *Ranching Traditions: Legacy of the American West*

Taking a break at a cattle round-up at the Huasna Ranch in Arroyo Grande
LONDIE PADELSKY

Heading the horses back to the barn on California's central coast   LONDIE PADELSKY

Feeding time for a mare and her colt at the Garcia Ranch near San Luis Obispo   LONDIE PADELSKY

Snow recedes from petroglyphs in the Chalfant Valley, but not from the peaks of the Sierra Nevada in the distance   DENNIS FLAHERTY

In the Providence Mountains Scenic Recreation Area, Mitchell Caverns' El Pakiva Cave
exhibits petrified stalactites and stalagmites   FRANK S. BALTHIS

The setting sun illuminates a geometric rock puzzle in Joshua Tree National Park   JEFF FOOTT

❝ We all remember our first trip to California. It is a place less western than mythic, and the elements of its landscape are firmly fixed in the American mind. Where else is geography wedded to fantasy? ❞

Bill Barich
from *Picturing California:*
A Century of Photographic Genius

Once one of the wildest mining towns in the West, Bodie is now a ghost town preserved for visitors in a state of "arrested decay" MIKE ANICH

A storefront in the ghost town of Calico; in 1881 it was the site of one of the West's richest silver strikes TOM TILL

On a clear October morning in Death Valley National Park, Tin Mountain rises behind Scotty's Castle, a desert mansion built by the eccentric Death Valley Scotty (Walter Scott) JEFF GNASS

Stanford University's Memorial Church, dedicated in 1903, was twice rebuilt after it suffered two major earthquakes that shook the San Francisco Bay Area KERRICK JAMES

The Crystal Cathedral in Garden Grove is surrounded by 32 acres of flowering gardens DENNIS SHIRTCLIFF/FREEZE FRAME WEST

The Mormon Temple is a spectacular La Jolla landmark DENNIS SHIRTCLIFF/FREEZE FRAME WEST

Yosemite Chapel in Yosemite National Park stands at the base of sheer rock walls   DENNIS FLAHERTY

Sailboats dot the bay and the sun bathes San Francisco's skyline: view from Tiburon, Marin County JAMES RANDKLEV

" . . . we began rolling in the foothills before Oakland and suddenly reached a height and saw stretched out ahead of us the fabulous white city of San Francisco on her eleven mystic hills with the blue Pacific and its advancing wall of potato-patch fog beyond, and smoke and goldenness in the late afternoon of time. "

Jack Kerouac
On The Road

Trimming the sails on windy San Francisco Bay   CHUCK PLACE

Victorian houses line neighborhood streets while the sparkling San Francisco skyline glimmers in the background   KATHLEEN NORRIS COOK

Evening commuters and tourists jump from a San Francisco cable car as it crests a hill
MARK E. GIBSON

Breakers on Baker Beach and a sunset-lit Golden Gate Bridge, the famous entrance to San Francisco Bay   JEFF GNASS

Keeping the Golden Gate Bridge, San Francisco's best-known landmark, spruced up and protected
from the elements is a continual task—not for the faint of heart   GALEN ROWELL/MOUNTAIN LIGHT

People and banners crowd Grant Avenue in San Francisco's Chinatown   KERRICK JAMES

Pier 39 on San Francisco's waterfront is a draw for tourists and sea lions   FRANK S. BALTHIS

A centerpiece for the 1915 Panama-Pacific International Exposition, San Francisco's Palace of Fine Arts
now houses the Exploratorium, a hands-on science museum   MARK E. GIBSON

The seiner "Maria Amalia" and her floats await their next voyage   STEPHEN SIMPSON

Once a haunt of writer John Steinbeck, Monterey's quiet Fisherman's Wharf casts a shadow on Pacific waters   KERRICK JAMES

Happy fishing boat skipper   DAN ROOT/BORLAND STOCK

" Cannery Row in Monterey in California is a poem, a stink, a grating noise, a quality of light, a tone, a habit, a nostalgia, a dream. "

John Steinbeck
Cannery Row

Sunset silhouettes Catalina Island while gulls rest at Newport Beach FRANK S. BALTHIS

*66 Like bits of foam on wing, flocks
of gulls curve and circle past the cliff
face. . . . Life is zestful here, out on
land's edge, with winging, calling
birds and spindrift blowing off a
swelling sea. 99*

Elna S. Bakker
An Island Called California

A western gull nesting on the Farallon Islands MICHAEL EVAN SEWELL

Common dolphins on a run through Pacific waters   BOB CRANSTON

A sea lion colony takes over a beach near Monterey   FRANK S. BALTHIS

Point Reyes National Seashore: the cliffs at Drake's Beach warm to a winter sunset   MICHAEL EVAN SEWELL

Young elephant seals, called weaners   FRANK S. BALTHIS

The Pacific Coast Highway (State Highway 1, California's most scenic route) hugs the Big Sur coastline
at Los Padres National Forest LARRY ULRICH

An alpine pond in Yosemite reflects its sunny surroundings   KATHLEEN NORRIS COOK

The historic Ahwahnee Hotel in Yosemite National Park was named for the Yosemite Valley's
original inhabitants, the Ahwahneechee Indians   FRANK S. BALTHIS

A cinnamon-colored black bear ART WOLFE

" California is big in an age that prizes bigness. "

Ralph J. Roske
Everyman's Eden: A History of California

Glimpses of Tenaya Lake and its glacial past surround this western white pine in Yosemite National Park   JEFF FOOTT

66 . . . the mighty Sierra, miles in height, reposing like a smooth, cumulus cloud in the sunny sky, and so gloriously colored, and so luminous, it seems to be not clothed with light, but wholly composed of it, like the wall of some celestial city. 99

John Muir
The Mountains of California

The face of Yosemite's El Capitan has challenged climbers for decades   LARRY ULRICH

Though it's not California's tallest mountain, 14,161-foot Mount Shasta is one of the most striking
and recognizable peaks in the Golden State MIKE HOUSKA/BORLAND STOCK

66 *Give me men to match my mountains.* 99

Sam Walter Foss
Inscription on the State Capitol—Sacramento

Cascade Falls near Lake Tahoe makes for a scenic obstacle
LARRY PROSOR

Mount Lassen, reflected here in the calm waters of Manzanita Lake, is the most recently active of California's volcanoes; it erupted numerous times between 1914 and 1917   WAYNE ALDRIDGE/BORLAND STOCK

An ice cave in Lassen Volcanic National Park LARRY CARVER

66 When a Californian boasts that his state has the highest mountain in the country, the lowest and hottest desert, the highest waterfall, the greatest bird, the most extensive vineyard, the biggest oranges, the tallest and oldest trees, he is stating a simple fact. California has infinite variety. 99

Roger Tory Peterson
Wild America

A mule deer buck descending a mountain meadow DONALD M. JONES

North Palisade Peak fades into evening in Kings Canyon National Park   ERIC WUNROW

A rainbow of color dwarfs this bungee-jumper in his descent from a hot-air balloon near Rancho Peñasquitos in San Diego County   ROB GILLEY

A young skateboarder defies gravity on a half pipe in Carlsbad   ROB GILLEY

One more creek reaches the ocean at McWay Falls in Julia Pfeiffer Burns State Park   FRANK S. BALTHIS

94

Nightfall in San Diego, where climate, people, and culture combine to make this southern California
city one of the nation's most livable STEPHEN SIMPSON

> *Although surrounded by people, attractions, and the beauty of San Diego's place and climate, the city still eludes me, defying specifics. It is a place that stays on your mind, but not of any mind that wants to categorize, size up, pin down, and move on.*

Peter Jensen
San Diego on My Mind

Teens in San Diego and their school-pride mural
STEPHEN SIMPSON

Beachside ambiance and nostalgia characterize the Hotel del Coronado in San Diego   CHRISTOPHER TALBOT FRANK

66 It is very easy to sit at the bar in, say, La Scala in Beverly Hills, or Ernie's in San Francisco, and to share in the pervasive delusion that California is only five hours from New York by air. The truth is that La Scala and Ernie's are only five hours from New York by air. California is somewhere else. 99

Joan Didion
Notes from a Native Daughter

Suspended for a moment in that magical place where land meets sea   STEPHEN SIMPSON

The Alcazar Gardens and the tower of the Museum of Man are two of the sights that distinguish San Diego's Balboa Park   PAULA BORCHARDT

Baseball fans pack cavernous 3Com Park—formerly Candlestick Park—to cheer on the San Francisco Giants MARK E. GIBSON

California's rich railroading history comes to life at the California
Railroad Museum in Sacramento KERRICK JAMES

Built between 1860 and 1874, California's stately Capitol is graced by fountains and a circle of roses   ED COOPER

A California rose and its edible hips   DAVID CAVAGNARO

Pussy ears at Point Reyes   DAVID CAVAGNARO

An oasis in the California desert, the Double Tree Country Club in Palm Springs is a top destination for golfers and other pleasure seekers
JAMES RANDKLEV

" The desert often seems monotonous, gray, and vast. . . . Coming suddenly upon a desert spring, then, is like finding an island in the ocean."

A. Starker Leopold
Wild California: Vanishing Lands, Vanishing Wildlife

Golf legend-in-the-making Tiger Woods during the AT&T Tournament at
Spyglass Hill Golf Club, Pebble Beach   FRANK S. BALTHIS

An ocotillo stands in the path of a spring thunderstorm in Anza-Borrego Desert State Park   CHRISTOPHER TALBOT FRANK

California quail, the state bird   ART WOLFE

Brittlebush blooms yellow under a clearing sky at Glorieta Canyon in Anza-Borrego Desert State Park   TERRY DONNELLY

Hearst Castle, fabled home of newspaper magnate William Randolph Hearst, is a top tourist attraction near San Simeon, along the southern reaches of scenic State Highway 1

Carson House, now a restored private club, was once home to a lumber baron in Eureka   JAMES RANDKLEV

A recreation of Ronald Reagan's Oval Office at his Presidential Library in Simi Valley
MARK E. GIBSON

Ken Bannister, the Banana Man, talks on a banana phone at the Banana Museum in Altadena   PAULA BORCHARDT

66 The American Dream is more alive in California than anywhere else. 99

Valeria Manferto De Fabianis
California

The Chiat Day ad agency building in Venice is worth a closer look   PAULA BORCHARDT

The Lion, the Tin Man, and the Scarecrow welcome in the New Year at Pasadena's Tournament of Roses Parade, an annual tradition that was started in 1890 by members of Pasadena's Valley Hunt Club DENNIS SHIRTCLIFF/FREEZE FRAME WEST

The Italian Street Painting Festival, held each year in Santa Barbara, gives artists a chance to showcase their talents DENNIS SHIRTCLIFF/FREEZE FRAME WEST

Once a hideout for buccaneers and smugglers, Catalina Island now draws visitors from the mainland (only 21 miles distant) to Avalon Harbor for sightseeing and recreation   KATHLEEN NORRIS COOK

American black oystercatcher   JEFF FOOTT

Brown pelican at Morro Bay State Park   LONDIE PADELSKY

<blockquote>

❝ When I am in California, I am not in the west,
I am west of the west. ❞

</blockquote>

Theodore Roosevelt

Draper Rock shelters two paddlers along the Colorado River at the Imperial National Wildlife Refuge   JACK W. DYKINGA

" The attraction and superiority of California are in its days.
It has better days, and more of them, than any other country. "

Ralph Waldo Emerson
Journal

The eastern Sierra Nevada provides a mighty backdrop for this hot-air balloonist
suspended above Sierra Lake, near the town of Mammoth Lakes LONDIE PADELSKY

Beauty by the bay: Mendocino beckons travelers along California's northern coast   LARRY PROSOR

Rhododendrons bloom amid stout trunks of coastal redwoods at
Redwood National Park near Crescent City   CHUCK PLACE

Julia Pfeiffer Burns State Park, a breathtakingly scenic stretch of California's world-famous central coastline   DENNIS FLAHERTY

Aspens begin to turn on Monument Ridge in Toiyabe National Forest   LARRY ULRICH

Autumn travel via backcountry pack train near North Lake in Bishop Canyon   LONDIE PADELSKY

The West Fork Carson River runs along the Carson Pass Highway Scenic Byway and the historic California Emigrant Trail   JEFF GNASS

Sand bars resemble fish in the shallows along the Colorado River in the Picacho State Recreation Area JACK DYKINGA

Pronghorn antelope DONALD M. JONES

Indianhead Falls sculpts a boulder in Borrego Palm Canyon in Anza-Borrego Desert State Park LARRY ULRICH

they made it possible

California on My Mind would have been impossible to produce without the keen eyes and technical skills of more than thirty-five professional photographers. These women and men submitted their finest images, and the results show in this stunning collection of photos. What does not show is the work it took to get these images— the early mornings to capture the sunrise, the long climbs through rugged terrain, the endless hours of waiting for the perfect light, the hundreds of shots that didn't turn out quite right, and the high level of technical skill that was acquired through years of experience and study. To all the photographers who contributed to *California on My Mind,* we say thanks. We appreciate their art and their hard work.

Michael S. Sample and Bill Schneider
Publishers, Falcon Press

Photographers in *California on My Mind*

Mike Anich

Frank S. Balthis

Paula Borchardt

Larry Carver

David Cavagnaro

Kathleen Norris Cook

Ed Cooper

Bob Cranston

Terry Donnelly

Jack Dykinga

Dennis Flaherty

Jeff Foott

Christopher Talbot Frank

James K. Gardner

Mark E. Gibson

Rob Gillety

Jeff Gnass

Kerrick James

Donald M. Jones

Steve Mohlenkamp

Londie G. Padelsky

Chuck Place

Larry Prosor

James Randklev

Cheyenne Rouse

Galen Rowell

Mike Sewell

Dennis Shirtcliff

Stephen Simpson

Tom Till

Larry Ulrich

Art Wolfe

Eric Wunrow

Gary Zahn

Borland Stock Photo
   Wayne Aldridge
   Mike Houskie
   Dan Root

Tom Stack & Associates
   Randy Morse

© 1997 by Falcon Press® Publishing Co., Inc.
Helena and Billings, Montana

All rights reserved, including the right to reproduce any part of this book in any form, except brief quotations for reviews, without the written permission of the publisher.

Design, typesetting, and other prepress work by Falcon Press, Helena, Montana.
Printed in Hong Kong

Library of Congress Number: 97-060379

ISBN 1-56044-570-X

For extra copies of this book please check with your local bookstore, or write Falcon Press, P.O. Box 1718, Helena, MT 59624 or call toll-free 1-800-582-2665.

Title page:
   Pinnacles National Moument LARRY CARVER

End papers:
   Palms along Harbor Drive, San Diego
   STEVE SIMPSON

acknowledgments

The publisher gratefully acknowledges the following sources:

Page 1 quoted in *Picturing California: A Century of Photographic Genius.* © 1989 by The Oakland County Museum; Chronicle Books, San Francisco.

Page 3 quoted in *Anza-Borrego Desert State Park* by Paul R. Johnson. © 1982 by Anza-Borrego Desert Natural History Association.

Page 6 from *An Island Called California: An Ecological Introduction to its Natural Communities* by Elna S. Bakker. ©1971 by the Regents of the University of California; University of California Press, Berkeley and Los Angeles.

Page 10 quoted in *West of the West: Imagining California,* edited by Leonard Michaels, David Reid, and Raquel Scherr. © 1989 by Leonard Michaels, David Reid, and Raquel Scherr; University of California Press, Berkeley and Los Angeles.

Page 15 from *The Mountains of California* by John Muir. Viking Penguin Inc., New York.

Page 19 quoted in *Fray Junípero Serra and the California Conquest* by Winifred E. Wise. © 1967 by Winifred E. Wise; Charles Scribner's Sons, New York.

Page 23 from *Southern California Country* by Carey McWilliams. © 1946 by Duell, Sloan & Pearce, New York.

Page 28 quoted in *West of the West: Imagining California,* edited by Leonard Michaels, David Reid, and Raquel Scherr. © 1989 by Leonard Michaels, David Reid, and Raquel Scherr; University of California Press, Berkeley and Los Angeles.

Page 31 quoted in *West of the West: Imagining California,* edited by Leonard Michaels, David Reid, and Raquel Scherr. © 1989 by Leonard Michaels, David Reid, and Raquel Scherr; University of California Press, Berkeley and Los Angeles.

Page 32 from *The Mysterious Lands: An Award-Winning Naturalist Explores the Four Great Deserts of the Southwest* by Ann Haymond Zwinger. © 1989 by Ann Haymond Zwinger; Truman Talley Books/ Plume, New York.

Page 34 quoted in *Mono Lake: Mirror of Imagination* by Dennis Flaherty and Mark A. Schlenz. Text © 1996 by Mark A. Schlenz; Companion Press, Santa Barbara.

Page 38 from *The Mountains of California* by John Muir. Viking Penguin Inc., New York.

Page 40 from *The American River.* © 1989 by the Wilderness Conservancy. Published by Protect American River Canyons, Auburn.

Page 43 quoted in *The Traveller's Dictionary of Quotations,* edited by Peter Yapp. © 1983 by Peter Yapp; Routledge, New York.

Page 46 from *The American River.* © 1989 by the Wilderness Conservancy. Published by Protect American River Canyons, Auburn.

Page 48 from *The Mountains of California* by John Muir. Viking Penguin Inc., New York.

Page 51 from *Southern California Country* by Carey McWilliams. © 1946 by Duell, Sloan & Pearce, New York.

Page 52 from *California From the Air: The Golden Coast* by Richard Reinhardt. © 1981 by Squarebooks; Chronicle Books, San Francisco.

Page 62 quoted in *Life on the Edge: A Guide to California's Endangered Natural Resources* by Carl G. Thelander and Margo Crabtree. © 1994 by Biosystems Analysis Inc., Santa Cruz.

Page 64 quoted in *Ranching Traditions: Legacy of the American West,* edited by Alan Axelrod. © 1979 by Cross River Press; Abbeville Publishing Groups, New York.

Page 67 quoted in *Picturing California: A Century of Photographic Genius.* © 1989 by The Oakland County Museum; Chronicle Books, San Francisco.

Page 73 quoted in *West of the West: Imagining California,* edited by Leonard Michaels, David Reid, and Raquel Scherr. © 1989 by Leonard Michaels, David Reid, and Raquel Scherr; University of California Press, Berkeley and Los Angeles.

Page 79 from *Cannery Row* by John Steinbeck. © 1945 by John Steinbeck; Bantam Books, New York.

Page 80 from *An Island Called California: An Ecological Introduction to its Natural Communities* by Elna S. Bakker. ©1971 by the Regents of the University of California; University of California Press, Berkeley and Los Angeles.

Page 85 from *Everyman's Eden: A History of California* by Ralph J. Roske. © 1968 by MacMillan, New York.

Page 86 from *The Mountains of California* by John Muir. Viking Penguin Inc., New York.

Page 88 quoted in *The Traveller's Dictionary of Quotations,* edited by Peter Yapp. © 1983 by Peter Yapp; Routledge, New York.

Page 90 from *Wild America* by Roger Tory Peterson. © 1935 by Roger Tory Peterson. Houghton Mifflin, Boston.

Page 95 from *San Diego on My Mind* by Peter Jensen. © 1989 by Falcon Press Publishing Co., Inc., Helena.

Page 96 quoted in *West of the West: Imagining California,* edited by Leonard Michaels, David Reid, and Raquel Scherr. © 1989 by Leonard Michaels, David Reid, and Raquel Scherr; University of California Press, Berkeley and Los Angeles.

Page 101 from *Wild California: Vanishing Lands, Vanishing Wildlife* by A. Starker Leopold. © 1985 by Elizabeth Leopold; University of California Press, Berkeley and Los Angeles.

Page 106 from *California* by Marcello and Angela Bertinetti. © 1985 by White Star Edizioni, Vercelli, Italy.

Page 109 quoted in *West of the West: Imagining California,* edited by Leonard Michaels, David Reid, and Raquel Scherr. © 1989 by Leonard Michaels, David Reid, and Raquel Scherr; University of California Press, Berkeley and Los Angeles.

Page 110 quoted in *The Traveller's Dictionary of Quotations,* edited by Peter Yapp. © 1983 by Peter Yapp; Routledge, New York.

Page 120 quoted in *West of the West: Imagining California,* edited by Leonard Michaels, David Reid, and Raquel Scherr. © 1989 by Leonard Michaels, David Reid, and Raquel Scherr; University of California Press, Berkeley and Los Angeles.

A special California moment makes for memories that last a lifetime   CHEYENNE ROUSE

*66 The usual word for California, the one that first rises to
the lips, is that it is a paradise. And that is true. 99*

Julián Marías
California as Paradise